D1088918

FOOTBALL

THOMAS S. OWENS
DIANA STAR HELMER

TWENTY-FIRST CENTURY BOOKS
BROOKFIELD, CONNECTICUT

To Kevin Whitver, with thanks

Cover photograph courtesy of R. Llewellyn/SuperStock

Photographs courtesy of Reuters/Archive Photos: pp. 8 (© Jason Cohn), 31 (© Ron Kuntz), 53 (© Ray Stubblebine); AP/Wide World Photos: pp. 9, 12, 13, 20, 24, 26; NFL Photos: pp. 15 (left © Michael Martin, right © James V. Biever), 22 (© Greg Crisp), 33 (© Michael Zagaris), 40 (© James F. Flores), 44 (© Allen Dean Steele), 50 (© Paul Spinelli); Allsport: pp. 27 (© Stephen Dunn), 37 (© Rick Stewart), 38 (© Jonathan Daniel), 47 (© Rick Stewart), 54 (© Andy Lyons)

Owens, Tom, 1960-
  Football / by Thomas S. Owens and Diana Star Helmer.
  p. cm. — (Game Plan)
  Includes index.
  Summary: Describes how professional football teams prepare for games, analyze the games afterwards for improvement, develop strategies, and build themselves through player selection.
  ISBN 0-7613-3233-2 (lib. bdg.)
  1. Football—United States—Juvenile literature. [1. Football.]
I. Helmer, Diana Star, 1962- . II. Title. III. Series: Owens, Tom, 1960- Game Plan.
GV954.094 1998
796.332'0973—dc21   98-26711 CIP
                    AC

Published by Twenty-First Century Books
A Division of The Millbrook Press, Inc.
2 Old New Milford Road
Brookfield, Connecticut 06804

CONTENTS

SUPER BOWL BOUND

A game plan is a map. But maps don't tell you everything.

Suppose you and your mom plan a trip to your first National Football League (NFL) game. You find your own town on the map. You find the city you want to go to, then you decide which roads will take you to the stadium. You mark those roads, hop in the car, and follow the directions until—

"Road closed for repairs?" Your mom pulls the car over and takes out the map. "Now we'll have to pick a new route. I swear they put up roadblocks just where they know they'll annoy me."

Which is exactly what's going to happen in the game, once you get there. Each team is going to have a plan mapped out, hoping to get to the winner's circle. Each team will encounter roadblocks, forcing it to change plans and pick a new strategy. And each team will put up roadblocks of its own, trying to stop its opponent.

And those roadblocks really are put up just to be annoying.

SUPER BOWL, ONE WIN AWAY

On January 11, 1998, the Denver Broncos and the Pittsburgh Steelers took the field in a game that would decide which team would advance to the Super Bowl.

It didn't look good for the Broncos.

This was the third time the Steelers had been in the playoffs in the previous four years. Two years before, Pittsburgh had made it all the way to the Super Bowl.

And, just one month before, the Steelers had blown the Broncos away in their only regular-season match. Pittsburgh quarterback Kordell Stewart called it "definitely my best game." Denver quarterback John Elway called it "a good old-fashioned butt-whipping, and we were on the wrong end."

Bronco cornerback Darrien Gordon thought he knew what went wrong.

"The last time, we didn't give them disguises as far as our looks," he said. Denver had played straight man-to-man, he said, giving Pittsburgh "easy reads." The Steelers knew which Bronco was going to cover which Steeler, trying to prevent a pass completion.

Today, back on the Steelers' home field, the Broncos knew what they needed to do. Denver was going to roll out a game plan that "mixed our defenses up quite a bit," said safety Steve Atwater. They were "hoping to confuse" Pittsburgh.

But as the clock ticked down to the end of the first half, Denver's plan didn't seem to be working. Denver had scored in the first quarter, but the Steelers had answered right back with a touchdown of their own, then another. The second quarter was almost half over before Denver finally squeaked out a field goal, making the score 14–10.

STOPPING THE STEELERS

The Steelers used that next first down to gain eight yards. Just two more yards, and they would get another first down. They were already at the Denver 35-yard line—another touchdown wasn't far off. Steeler quarterback Stewart decided to go for it now.

"When you have the 'Bus' back there, you can take a shot on second and two," Bronco cornerback Ray Crockett said. The "Bus" he was talking about was 243-pound Pittsburgh running back Jerome Bettis. "If you don't make it, you still have the 'Bus' to try another play," Crockett said.

Knowing how Pittsburgh relied on Bettis, Crockett and the other Broncos watched quarterback Stewart and the rest of the Steeler offense. Sure enough, Pittsburgh took field formations that looked like a pass was coming. The Broncos quit guarding the zones, or areas of the field, they had been assigned. Instead, they scrambled to cover individual Pittsburgh players. Crockett's man was Steeler wide receiver Yancey Thigpen, and he pulled down a juicy interception. Denver's possession opened the door for a touchdown, and the half ended with the Broncos ahead.

> · · · · · · · · · · · · · · ·
> On December 31, 1967, Wisconsin provided 13-below-zero weather with a windchill factor of 50 below, turning the playoff between Dallas and Green Bay into a game later called "The Ice Bowl."

Denver's game plan had started to work, mixing up "zone, zone blitz, playing our corners up sometimes, just giving them different looks," cornerback Gordon said.

They kept it up in the second half. Pittsburgh quarterback Kordell Stewart, looking for man-to-man coverage from the Broncos, thought he saw a hole in their defense. He sent a pass flying for a score on a second down. But the ball dropped into the waiting hands of Bronco middle linebacker Allen Aldridge: Denver had switched to zone.

"Stewart really didn't know where to go," Denver safety Steve Atwater said.

Defensive end Neil Smith said, "We had a great game plan."

RAINY DAYS MAKE DIRTY PLAYS

That same January 11, two other teams were fighting it out for the final spot in the Super Bowl. Things didn't look good for either team.

The San Francisco 49ers were facing the Super Bowl champion Green Bay Packers. The year before, on a muddy Green Bay field, the Packers had bulldozed the 49ers. The Packers played well on a sloppy field, but not the 49ers. And it was raining again.

True, the Packers didn't mind the grime, but the Packers were playing on San Francisco's home field. Teams often play better at "home."

Denver Broncos running back Terrell Davis carries the ball past Pittsburgh Steelers Chad Scott to pick up a first down during Denver's drive to run out the clock. In this game for the AFC championship on January 11, 1998, the Broncos beat the Steelers 24–21 to advance to Super Bowl XXXII.

True, the Packers had allowed their opponents an average of just one touchdown per game for their last six games. Green Bay's defense was good—but San Francisco's defense was ranked the best in the league. And San Francisco's offense had quarterback Steve Young, known for his smartness, passing skills, and agility.

Worst of all for the Packers, the 49ers had two coaches who had recently worked for Green Bay. San Francisco had inside information on game plans the Packers used.

That's why Green Bay defensive coordinator Fritz Shurmur decided to "load up the wagon pretty good." He had the Packers defense use four defensive linemen. Then he told them to switch to three. Sometimes Shurmur called for four linebackers on a play; sometimes he

> **How did Green Bay get its name? A local meat-packing company sponsored the club, paying some bills in 1919.**

wanted just one. But Shurmur always had a linebacker cover quarterback Young. That forced Young to get rid of the ball and not scramble with it himself. The idea was to keep San Francisco guessing. And that kept San Francisco from scoring.

The Green Bay Packers won the NFC championship on January 11, 1998, when they defeated the San Francisco 49ers 23–10. Here Packers safety Eugene Robinson tries to dodge 49ers tight end Brent Jones after intercepting a pass.

TIME FOR OFFENSE

But the Packers still had to score. Their coach, Mike Holmgren, told the Green Bay *Press-Gazette*, "One of the keys to give us a chance to win was our ability to run well." Sometimes, running well means running when you can. Running back Dorsey Levens's longest carry of the day was 12 yards. Many were much shorter, but Levens finished the day with 100 yards. And the Green Bay Packers finished the day with another win, 23–10, which gave them another spot in the Super Bowl.

"We're doing better than we were last year," Shurmur said. "We're doing it differently, but we're doing it better."

Green Bay safety LeRoy Butler said, "No question about it. Denver's 1B, and we're 1A. The two best teams are in the Super Bowl."

But each team still had one more game plan to make.

SOME ASSEMBLY REQUIRED

The 1997 Denver Broncos were champions of the American Football Conference (AFC), and the Green Bay Packers were champions of the National Football Conference (NFC), because of their records and playoff wins. Because they were champions, the teams had a lot in common. Even the two head coaches, each named Mike, seemed alike.

Green Bay's Mike Holmgren had been the starting quarterback on his high-school team. So had Denver's Mike Shanahan. Each Mike had worked as offensive coordinator for the San Francisco 49ers before getting a head-coaching job. And as coaches, both used a way of playing that the 49ers made famous—the "West Coast offense," which featured a variety of quick, short passes.

The two Mikes had even faced each other in a previous Super Bowl. In Super Bowl XXIV, Holmgren led the 49ers' offense, while Shanahan was in charge of Denver's offense, featuring John Elway as quarterback. The result was a record-setting 55–10 win for San Francisco—and Shanahan wanted to

> When the American Football League merged with the NFL for the 1970 season, the Steelers, Cleveland Browns, and Baltimore Colts joined the AFL teams, making the American Football Conference (AFC).

Green Bay Packers head coach Mike Holmgren expresses disbelief at an official's call. Holmgren is wearing a modern headset that allows him to give instructions to his quarterback, who has a one-way radio speaker in his helmet. The speaker must be shut off 15 seconds before each play.

know how it happened. When Holmgren left San Francisco in 1992 to become head coach of the Packers, Shanahan took Holmgren's place as the offensive coordinator of the 49ers. By 1995, Shanahan was a head coach, too, back with the Denver Broncos.

THEIR TEAMS, THEIR WAYS

That's why both coaches liked the West Coast–style offense. But each coach had to make that style work for his own particular players. And that's where the two title-winning teams started to look very different.

Coaches don't always have much of a choice in the players they have to work with. Only a few head coaches have gained the additional job of general manager (GM). The general manager is the team owner's most powerful assis-

> "He can take his'n and beat your'n, and he can take your'n and beat his'n."
>
> —*That's how coach Bum Phillips honored rival coach Don Shula, whose 347 wins set an NFL record.*

tant. The GM can say which players are drafted, traded for, or signed from other teams as free agents. The GM decides how much players and coaches will be paid.

Green Bay entered Super Bowl XXXII with 25 players they had drafted over the years. Each of these players had never been paid to play football until Green Bay chose them. The 1997 Packers also got 4 players from trades with other teams and 23 from free agency. Free-agent players are professional players looking for a new place to work. Finally, Green Bay got nose tackle Gilbert Brown "off waivers." Brown's previous team, the Vikings, "waived" its right to his contract in 1993. That meant it lost Brown's services— but it didn't have to pay him, either! Other teams take turns deciding if they want to sign players on waivers. Green Bay agreed to pay Brown the amount the Vikings had been paying, taking Brown off waivers.

Denver Broncos head coach Mike Shanahan yells from the sideline during the AFC championship game against the Steelers. In August 1998 he signed a new seven-year contract with the Broncos.

IS OLDER BETTER?

Unlike Denver, Green Bay had signed older free-agents in the "twilight" of their careers, players like defensive end Reggie White and safety Eugene Robinson. These men in their 30s wouldn't play forever, but, as established stars, they might help their new team win it all sooner.

Denver's squad consisted of 32 free-agent players, 17 acquired through the draft and 3 from trades. Oddly, neither team had a starting quarterback discovered and drafted by its own organization. The Broncos had traded two players to the Baltimore Colts for Elway in 1983. Green Bay got quarterback Brett Favre in 1992 by letting the Atlanta Falcons use Green Bay's first pick in the upcoming draft.

No matter how a team approaches a player, every player still has to negotiate a contract. The player and team owners must agree on what the team will pay the player, and what the player must do to earn that money. When a player signs a contract, he agrees to do what his team says for a certain number of years. After three years of professional experience, any unsigned player becomes a "restricted" free agent. New teams can make the player an offer, but if his old team matches the offer, it is entitled to keep him. If the old team decides to let the restricted free agent leave, it will be awarded a later draft choice to make up for the loss. After four years, a player can be an unrestricted free agent, free to accept any team's offer.

Finally, a team can keep the right to re-sign three "transition players" and one "franchise" player every year. A franchise player is a star that people think of when they think of the team—for example, the 1997 Broncos' John Elway. As long as Denver paid Elway the average salary the league's top five quarterbacks received, no other team could hire Elway away, even for a higher price. The same rule applies to transition players, except that they are compared with 10 players. Transition players are team members of extra importance.

MANAGING THE MONEY

Building the Broncos and Packers into winners began long before the players took the field. The general managers of both teams had been picking talent for years before they hired coaches Holmgren and Shanahan.

Denver's GM, John Beake, was in his twelfth season when the Broncos went to Super Bowl XXXII. Beake had worked in many jobs for the team over the course of 28 years.

Beake's Green Bay counterpart, GM Ron Wolf, was part of the Oakland Raiders "front office" for 25 years before he became the Packers' executive vice president/general manager in 1991. Wolf not only got a big title—he got a big boss, too. The Packers are the only team owned by shareholders. Fans throughout the world can become owners of the team just by buying shares of stock.

Even the bosses have bosses. The National Football League makes rules for teams and team owners to follow. One of the trickiest rules for a GM is the salary cap. Since 1994, the league has limited the amount of money a team can spend each year to pay players. By seeing that every team spends the same on salaries, the NFL hopes that teams can be close in their levels of talent. Well-matched teams will play exciting games that give fans their money's worth.

A general manager is a vital part of any team and often brings years of experience to the position. Here are Broncos GM John Beake (left) and Packers GM Ron Wolf (right).

The NFL's team-building philosophies can work anywhere. Jack Youngblood began a 14-year career as a defensive star with the 1971 Los Angeles Rams. Now, as the vice president of the Orlando Predators of the Arena Football League, he sees a basic formula for an organization's success.

"As a franchise, the strength comes from the top and trickles down," Youngblood says. "We have had strong ownership groups and our head coach . . . has been very successful assembling players who can play together. Sometimes, it's easy to bring in good-caliber players, but the trick is making them play as a team."

A WINNING COMBINATION

3

"By invitation only."

It takes more than talent or desire to get into the NFL—you need an invitation, usually to the "Combines." At the Combines, teams share their basic scouting information. They also share the cost of bringing players to one location. That way, many teams can take a closer look at a wider range of top players.

Once a year, before the NFL's April draft, National Football Scouting (NFS) sponsors a day of physical and mental tests. Close to 300 college players are invited to these examinations early each spring. Passing the test is tough. But passing up the invitation to this event could spell doom to a college player's future in the NFL. Teams who might have millions of dollars waiting for young talent want to see those test results before making any big decisions.

SURVIVING THE COMBINES

NFL players who remember the experience often describe these scouting sessions in two words: "meat market." College athletes come to be tested in weight lifting, running, and other physical skills. Everything down to a player's teeth and the size of his skull are studied. Lastly, a timed written test is given to test the intelligence of aspiring NFL players.

> In 1959, only 12 NFL teams existed. Each team had 33 players, 396 total. In 1997, 30 teams had 47-man rosters, making jobs for 1,410 players.

These inspections aren't public—in the beginning. However, reporters hang around the Hoosierdome in Indianapolis for the February session. What players do they see coming or going? Will a team official give them a hint about the findings?

Findings from the Combines don't remain secret for long. By combining the results of all the tests for each player, ratings are developed. *USA TODAY* prints yearly "draft rating system" numbers, much as it prints listings for the value of Wall Street stocks. The newspaper claims the following scores indicate that a player rating

- 8.0–8.9 should be a first-year starter.
- 7.0–7.9 should develop into a future starter.
- 6.0–6.9 should be included on some team's roster, maybe as a substitute.
- 5.0–5.9 has enough potential to help a club somehow.

But scouting combines aren't the only sources that teams rely on for good information. A player's agent can tell interested teams when and where his client will be working out. Or a team might invite a few possible draft picks to work out at a special location to be observed—and judged—to a greater extent.

PROBING THE PERSONALITY

It takes more than athletic skill to be a good team player. That's why teams want to know about the attitudes of their future players. Any question might reveal something about a college player's ideas or habits. Prior to the 1998 draft, *USA TODAY* asked possible draft picks about the strangest questions they had heard from NFL team representatives. Some examples given were:

- Do you prefer baths or showers?
- Would you rather eat an apple or an orange?
- Can you put a worm on a fishing hook?

The last question might have been the trickiest. A team was hoping to find out not only how tough a player was but also if he had "dexterity," the ability to use his hands for detailed jobs. If he could grab a slippery worm, maybe he could grab a fumble squirting across the field.

One team asked a former University of Iowa guard who would win a fist fight between himself and Ross Verba. (Verba was a former Iowa teammate who had become a rookie star with the Green Bay Packers.) Another possible draftee said the New York Giants asked him to complete a 500-question test. Teams are trying harder than ever to learn about the bodies and minds of future players.

TAKING TURNS

The two-day draft is like a game in itself. All 30 teams take turns through seven rounds of selecting college players they would like to sign to contracts. When a team chooses a player, it has the sole right to sign a contract with him. No other teams can contact him. The NFL teams with the worst records from the previous season get the first picks. The Super Bowl winner, presumably the best team, picks last. Champions aren't supposed to need new players as badly as teams they have beaten!

When all the teams have chosen once, that's the end of the "first round." The draft is organized to be fair to everyone. But sometimes, in actual drafts, it seems as if some teams get more picks. Teams make draft deals with each other all through the year. If an NFL team thinks it has enough young talent, it might trade its draft pick for already-

Dallas Cowboys quarterback Troy Aikman played high-school football in Henryetta, Oklahoma. His team was known as the "Fighting Hens." Fans from other towns would tease Aikman's team, throwing rubber chickens on the field.

established players. "We'll trade you our spot in the first round for your running back." These agreements, or "compensatory draft selections," can account for 20 to 50 of the 250 picks, especially at the end of the draft.

VIEWING THE CHOOSING

Believe it or not, TV broadcasters love the draft. Fans of some teams will gather at stadiums to watch their team make draft choices. They'll watch and cheer for the future talent, as if the draft is the first game of the year.

The event is telecast live. Networks like ESPN will show team "war rooms." There, an NFL team's scouts, coaches, owners, and general

Four of the top five 1998 NFL first-round draft picks and the teams that selected them are (left to right) Curtis Enis, Chicago Bears; Ryan Leaf, San Diego Chargers; Peyton Manning, Indianapolis Colts; and 1997 Heisman Trophy winner Charles Woodson, Oakland Raiders. Woodson is the only primarily defensive player to win this college trophy.

manager—sometimes as many as 30 people—will huddle. Their discussions may look or sound wild as the team's staff debates whom to pick next. That's because teams have to be ready with more than one name for every round. After all, if a player is really special, another team could pick him first.

Teams start looking at available college players months before the draft, going to see them play at their schools. One of the traps of judging college talent is thinking that players from the best college teams should be chosen first. San Diego Chargers general manager Bobby Beathard issued this warning: "There are a lot of highly rated guys that may be very ordinary, but are in a system [on a team] that makes them look better than they are." Carl Peterson, Kansas City Chiefs general manager, agreed: "We have a saying: 'This player's as good as he's going to be.' " Teams want a player whose talents will grow over time in the NFL, not lessen or stay the same.

SEEING THE UNSEEN

How much scouting and study do teams really need before the draft? Indianapolis Colts general manager Bill Polian said: "You can only talk to so many people, so many times, without all of it becoming a blur....At some point in time, you have to arrive at your own conclusions. There are short-range and long-range plans: Who's going to be better faster, or who's going to be better down the road. All of those things play into your ultimate decision."

So does knowing that the NFL can't always rank a player's future by his looks. For example, consider Tim Lester, a star rusher at a smaller college (Eastern Kentucky University). Though he was 5 foot 10 and 233 pounds, scouts still thought he was too small to be a fullback and too slow to be a tailback.

But Lester worked hard enough to land a spot on the Los Angeles Rams practice squad. (Practice squads work out with the "real" team, but don't suit up for games.) When the coaches saw Lester's dedication, they promoted him to the active roster, allowing him to substitute in 11 games. Lester didn't earn a single rushing attempt. The Rams released

Although smaller than most pro football players, Tim Lester has proved his worth to the Steelers. Here we see him in action in a 1997 game.

him in 1995, but the Steelers picked him up the same year. The Steelers had seen Lester play for Los Angeles, and liked the way he handled blocking duties for Jerome Bettis. A year later, when Bettis joined Pittsburgh as a free agent, Lester kept blocking, leading Bettis through holes in the defensive line.

Despite all the tests and computers, there is no way to measure heart. A player's courage and fortitude can only be judged on the playing field.

CAMP IS NO VACATION

Less than one week after the April draft, most NFL teams begin their season preparation. These early workouts are called "minicamps," but the events are major in importance.

Rookie players make their first on-field appearance as members of the team that chose them. An undrafted player who has a chance of getting a contract from the team could be there, too. Teams will average 70 players in camp, far more than the 47 kept on the roster during the regular season. Fans and the media are sometimes allowed at football camp, too; they come eager for a sneak peek at the chosen talent.

Just like the "coming events" film before the movie at the theater, the minicamp gives big hints about which players could be regulars in the coming season. Running and conditioning are the main goals of these workouts, which often last three or four days. But coaches also get their first chance to assemble some of the newest team members, seeing how the individuals look as a group.

MINICAMPS, MINI WORRIES

Veterans don't worry as much about minicamps. They know that bench-pressing lots of weight or turning in top sprint times won't guarantee new draftees a job. Head-to-head contact and scrimmages are how

Indianapolis Colts quarterback Peyton Manning (left) and running back Marshall Faulk stretch before the start of practice at a minicamp in April 1998. Manning was the first pick in the NFL draft just the week before.

experienced NFL players judge newcomers and their abilities to survive an entire season.

Defensive end Karl Lorch remembered getting drafted by the Miami Dolphins after finishing at the University of Southern California in 1973. "Miami had gone 17–0 the year before. When [head coach Don] Shula arrived at minicamp, he said: 'Most of you will get cut when the veterans arrive, because we really don't need anyone.' At that point, I said to myself, 'If that's the case, what am I doing here?'" Lorch left the minicamp before the Dolphins could tell him to leave. He went on to play six years for the Washington Redskins.

Sometimes the minicamps seem like checkups, at other times like semester tests. Some teams hold only one minicamp. Others hold as many as four separate sessions, some for rookies, some for veterans, stretching into June. In the "old days," NFL football players were paid so little that many felt they had to work off-season jobs. Spring camps were necessary for physical conditioning back then. Today's players can, and often do, spend the off-season working out, staying in top physical shape with personalized weight and exercise programs. But even though today's players usually arrive at camp in fine physical condition, coaches want to know what kind of personal training each player has been doing, and if he's following previous orders given by coaches. Have the player's weight and health improved or worsened since last season? Have game injuries healed?

Even before training camp, some players are asked to serve in the spring NFL Europe League. For ten weeks, from April through June, teams play in Germany, Spain, Scotland, the Netherlands, and England. Their season concludes with the World Bowl. NFL teams may assign prospective draftees, players recovering from injuries, or former players wanting another chance to European clubs, to display their skills in real games.

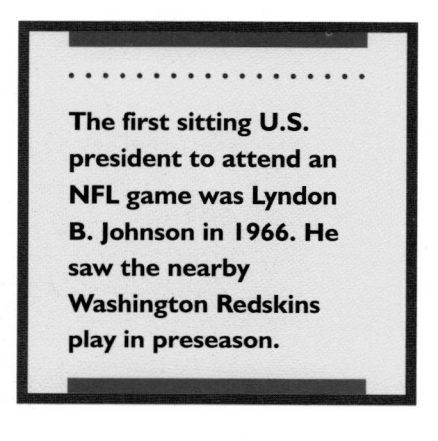

The first sitting U.S. president to attend an NFL game was Lyndon B. Johnson in 1966. He saw the nearby Washington Redskins play in preseason.

Actual training camps begin from mid-July to early August, and they last from four to six weeks. Many clubs train at colleges in Wisconsin, which have fewer students in the summer. These teams are jokingly called "The Cheese League," after Wisconsin's dairy industry.

PRESEASON PROBLEMS

These preseason workouts can have a big impact on the coming season. For example, scrimmages and contact practices can result in injuries, just like actual games. But if a player gets hurt before the

Duane Ashman (right) and teammate Nate Cochran celebrate their team's victory at the 1998 World Bowl in Frankfurt, Germany. They played for the Duesseldorf Rhein Fire team.

season, the team still has to pay the money it promised—without spending any more money on other players. The "salary cap" means that each team gets only so much money a year to pay players.

That's why, in 1994, Kansas City Chiefs head coach Marty Schottenheimer decided to reduce the number of scrimmages and contact practice in training. He was trying to prevent injuries before the season. Surprisingly, the care didn't pay off. Injuries doubled *during* the season because players weren't conditioned to the wear and tear of game situations.

Training camp can't match the conditions of the real season, but the closer it comes, the better. The Dallas Cowboys used to train in Michigan. Then they switched to California. Today they train in Texas. Why? The shoe-melting humid weather the Cowboys have for home games is unlike that of any other place.

A Dallas Cowboys training camp often attracts a number of spectators in spite of the heat.

The daytime training-camp workouts may be open to the public. In the evenings, current and future members of a team keep working, though fans and reporters are not allowed to observe. Reviewing videos of the afternoon practice sessions and discussing the playbook can take several hours. New plays to be practiced the next day will be explained. How fast, and how well, can these newcomers learn and master so many plays? The players may not escape until 10 P.M. The coaching staff will continue alone, sometimes past midnight. One of their ongoing jobs is creating the team's "depth chart."

When coaches talk about being "four deep" at wide receiver, that means they have four players ready to play that spot. But, if the season started today, who would start at each position? If a person was injured, who would substitute? Of course, as a player, you want to move up the depth chart by showing your talent and desire in camp. But just "making the team"—with any job—is the biggest concern before the season starts.

Raiders quarterback-kicker George Blanda retired in August 1976. At age 48 years 11 months, he was the oldest-ever active player in the NFL.

Building depth charts can lead to "cuts"—players who aren't kept on the team roster. The first reports about training camp usually involve cuts. Being cut doesn't mean the player is washed up; in fact, a "cut" player may be invited by another team to come to its training camp. Of course, cut players are required to return their playbooks before leaving training camp.

PLAYING FOR POSITIONS

All the tests and training are leading up to preseason games, which will dot the final month of training camp. NFL teams play each other with their new, expanded rosters. The number of players on each team's active roster will be trimmed gradually to 47 before the season actually begins. But some lucky players from training camp may be kept for a practice squad, the team's first source of substitutes for injured players.

Other hopefuls might find that the best way to show their future talent to the coach is to accept one of the many jobs on a "special teams" unit for punts, kickoffs, or field goals.

Mike Donohoe's career with the Atlanta Falcons and Green Bay Packers lasted from 1968 through 1974. "The reason I made it in the pros," he said, "and the reason I stayed around for as long as I did, was I did everything the coaches asked. Which was anything and everything. To stay in the game with the limited talent I had, I think that said a lot about me as a person. I was smart enough to survive. I was very coachable."

While no professional player is guaranteed health or even employment by a team throughout the season, he's still a winner. After all, he has won the chance to be a member of the National Football League.

> "My greatest skill was paying attention to why things happen and not just 'what happened.' Also being able to concentrate on what is important."
>
> —Dave Casper, tight end, 1974–1984, five-time Pro Bowl selection

5 WORK BEFORE PLAY

Fans mainly see players in action on Sunday afternoons or Monday nights. But professional football is far from part-time work. The public doesn't get many looks at the physical and mental practice that goes on every week before each gridiron matchup throughout the season.

After the first game, the whole team has two huge tasks: review and preview. Some teams will take off the day after a game to rest and recover from the game's pounding. Others will come in that day for individual weight lifting, conditioning, and checkups, then take the following day off. However, by Wednesday, the past becomes the present, as all players and coaches watch videos of the previous contest before returning to the field for a practice.

John Madden, coach of the Oakland Raiders' Super Bowl XI championship team, put the philosophy of reviewing game video simply. "We watch the good things you do so you can see why and how you did them," he would tell players. "We watch the average things so you can improve on them, and we watch the bad things you do so you won't do them again."

SEEING IS BELIEVING

Players have mixed feelings about reviewing their past mistakes. Mike Webster was the center for four Pittsburgh Steelers Super Bowl winners in the 1970s, gaining Hall of Fame membership in 1997. "Teams get it all down on game film. We'd never go to sleep after a game till we'd watch the films," he said. "We'd let the new guys hang themselves when the coach asked, 'What happened out there?' and the new guys would say, 'Well, this and this....' The coach would say, 'Oh, really?' then run the film. I learned never to say anything till after we'd seen the film and I'd taken notes on every play."

In the end, every player has to discover how technology serves him best. Today, some players view game tapes on their own time, in addition to team sessions. And not all coaches agree that the key to winning is in constant review of videos. Bud Grant served as Minnesota Vikings head coach from 1967 to 1983, returning in 1985. In 1994 he was elected to the Hall of Fame. "As head coach, I could see most of what went on

Head coaches may work in various ways to develop a winning record. Four-time Super Bowl coach Bud Grant (third from left) is shown here when he was inducted into the Pro Football Hall of Fame in 1994. The others inducted at the same time are (left to right) Leroy Kelly, Tony Dorsett, Jimmy Johnson, Jackie Smith, and Randy White.

during practice. I had a good feel for what was working and what wasn't working and why," he said. "I did not need to chart every down and distance situation, document every play, and go back and check it against the film."

Norv Turner became the offensive coordinator of the Dallas Cowboys in 1991. "I cut the offense down by about 70 percent and retained only those plays and formations that allowed the guys to do what they could do best," he says. Turner explains that the old offensive playbook was too complicated, asking players to do too many jobs. The Cowboys felt happier, doing what they could do best. Turner slowly added a few new plays. Within two years, Dallas won Super Bowls XXVII and XXVIII.

> A halfback-option pass lets a running back choose to throw to a receiver. Walter Payton of the Chicago Bears mastered the play, throwing eight TD passes in his career.

Still, many head coaches would sleep at their stadium offices during the week, watching films endlessly. Many would have offensive and defensive coordinators at their sides. These are the coaches for the coaches.

PLAYING ON PAPER

Bill Walsh was head coach of the San Francisco 49ers from 1979 to 1988, winning three Super Bowls and six division titles. Walsh learned his skills as an offensive assistant for coaches Al Davis of the Oakland Raiders and Paul Brown of the Cincinnati Bengals in the late 1960s and early 1970s. Brown's coaching unit developed "scripting"—diagramming plays and the order they would be used in. Other teams, then and now, relied on a list of plays to select from for certain downs or yardage-needed situations.

But no matter what the game plan, players will study every phase of it. The offense will meet with its coaches. The defense and its coaches will plot. Even special teams will discuss how to handle field goals, as well as kickoffs, punts, and returns of both.

By Thursday, coaches are required to turn in an injury list to the NFL office. And, of course, the media will be pressing the coach to name the starters. All this lets opponents have some idea which players they will be facing. If a coach knows the lineup the other team will field, his players can view videos of those specific players. Most coaches use their pregame afternoons to review trouble spots, or overlooked details, such as the kick for the extra point (point after touchdown).

A supporting cast helps each team before and during games. Strength and conditioning coaches work to prevent injuries by keeping players fit and flexible. Trainers, who aren't always doctors, try to help players care for bruises, sore muscles, or slow-healing injuries. They work with equipment managers to see that pads, helmets, and other gear are repaired and ready to protect the players.

The San Francisco 49ers' assistant head coach makes good use of a chalkboard at half time to analyze a play.

THE EYES IN THE SKY

On game day, the coaching staff plans their team's battle positions. Some assistants watch from the press box during games, where they can view the entire field from above. They phone advice down to the field. A one-way radio speaker is in the quarterback's helmet. He can hear one sideline coach but is unable to talk back. League rules require that the radio be shut off 15 seconds before each play.

Teams get visual help, too, using video printers. Coaches can review thermofax photos of the previous series of plays, getting views from the end zone and the 50-yard line seconds after the event. If a team can see proof of what it did wrong, the coaches can make instant corrections.

And teams don't stop their game planning once the game starts. Timeouts (three per half) and halftime give the coaches additional chances to fix mistakes or change plays.

Whenever coach Bill Walsh and his 49ers were leaving to play on a "foreign" field, he would try to convince his players that playing away from home may have advantages. After all, "We just have to be here for three hours and then we can go home," he'd say with a grin. "They gotta live here."

PLAN THE UNEXPECTED

At one time, a coach could explain his plans for future plays on a chalkboard, marking the positions of all 22 offensive and defensive players with X's and O's. On the field, his quarterback would size up the opponent's defense formation and have a chance to devise a better plan in the seconds before the ball was snapped.

But that was then. "Everything is called nowadays," said Karl Lorch, who played for the Washington Redskins from 1976 to 1981. "The offense is called, the defense is called. There is no freedom of expression. We had [quarterbacks] Billy Kilmer and Sonny Jurgensen and, well, they'd get out there and almost draw plays in the dirt. Nowadays, they [teams] have earphones in the helmets and [coaches] are calling the plays from the press box." Lorch doesn't account for quarterbacks changing the play at the line with an "audible" call. But even though play-calling in the huddle is a dying art, basic communication between team members still keeps offenses clicking. And that communication hasn't changed much over time.

RECEIVERS' GAME PLAN

Wide receiver Carroll Dale and his Green Bay Packers won Super Bowl I in 1967, thanks in part to Dale's league-leading 23.7 yards gained per catch.

"The quarterback and receivers would talk on the sidelines and sometimes while on the field. The receivers would tell the QBs that [the defense] might be overplaying a route, or that they were too close or that they might be playing hard outside, hard inside or extremely loose," Dale recalls. Even if a receiver hadn't touched the ball, what they learned about defensive coverage on each play could help the quarterback choose his future pass targets or alter patterns to be run by possible receivers.

"I guess that present-day receivers would have to talk with the coach between series now," Dale added. "The coaches now call all the plays instead of the QBs of our day."

On November 8, 1970, place-kicker Tom Dempsey of the New Orleans Saints set a record with a 63-yard field goal. Dempsey was born without a right hand and with only part of a right foot.

THE FRONT LINE

No matter who calls the plays, the plan won't work unless every team member understands the goals of the team's offense. "On offense, there is a lot more to think about—more study is required," said Tom Randall, an offensive guard with the 1978 Dallas Cowboys and 1979 Houston Oilers. "I played defense at Iowa State, so this was quite a change. The Dallas Cowboy playbook that we received was thicker than any textbook I've ever seen. In the beginning, I lost some of my aggressiveness, because I was having to think too much about what I was supposed to be doing. As my confidence in my assignments grew, so did the aggressiveness which was necessary to excel."

But Green Bay's Ross Verba said, "I never really look at it as pressure." Playing left tackle at 6 foot 4 and nearly 300 pounds, he became the first rookie starter in a Super Bowl for the 1997 Packers. "I just know that I'm about five feet away from Brett [Favre] being decapitated, so I just block my guy and try to keep him away from the quarterback."

Verba concentrated most on the basic goal of the offense: For any play, the quarterback needs time and protection. "The goal was to not allow a quarterback sack or hit," agreed offensive guard Randall, but

A play diagram may be reviewed on the sidelines during a game to be sure an upcoming play is clear to the players, or perhaps to analyze a play that didn't work.

added that coaches judge guards by "movement at the line of scrimmage—was I moving forward or backward—footwork, explosion off the ball, body position— I was judged by my overall techniques."

POCKETING A QUARTERBACK

Two guards (like Randall), two tackles (like Verba), and a center are the fivesome that can form a human wall and create a "pocket," an area of safety from which a quarterback can throw a pass. The pocket gives the quarterback valuable seconds to size up the defense's field positions and find an open man, or men, for the pass. (The first receiver may be covered.)

The "West Coast offense" popularized by the 1980s San Francisco 49ers depends on an assortment of short passes. But whether the offense favors a "running game" or a "passing game," running backs, re-

The main job of Packers tackle Ross Verba (right) is to keep the opposition away from the quarterback. Here he blocks Marcellus Wiley of the Buffalo Bills in a December 1997 game that the Packers won 31–21.

ceivers, and tight ends are expected to help out with blocks, too. The best ground gainers need more than speed and sure hands.

Houston Oilers running back Earl Campbell led the NFL in rushing for a third-straight season in 1980, making his 1,934 yards rushed the second-best mark in history at that time. Defenders bunched up near the 5-foot-11, 233-pound Campbell. Tackling him was a group outing: Campbell could drag opponents with him as he kept running. "I've learned how to give a guy a shoulder, how to give a leg and take it away and use a stiff arm now and then," he said.

DOING THE UNEXPECTED

Each offensive player has a different job, but they all have the same goal—*winning*. Most fans know Denver quarterback John Elway, especially after his team's Super Bowl XXXII championship. But only the most devoted fans remember Elway's brief fame as a pass receiver. In Denver's 1986 home opener, running back Steve Sewell took a handoff from Elway. Elway ran a pattern and hooked up for a 23-yard touchdown in a reversal that stunned the visiting Raiders. The touchdown made the difference as the Broncos shocked Oakland, 38–36.

In the current NFL, it isn't enough for a team to have great plays. If opposing teams know your team has been depending on a few basic offensive plays throughout the year, a "trick" play may be the ticket. The key here is to have as many players as possible doing the unexpected. One famed example is the "flea-flicker," a term used to describe tricky plays such as a handoff to a running back, passed underhand right back to the QB. The fake run supposedly baffles the defense. It's time for a surprise pass, the longer the better!

> In 1981 the NFL out-lawed receivers from applying sticky substances on their hands to help in catching balls.

In Super Bowl I in January 1967, the Packers and Chiefs were tied 7–7. On third down, needing only one yard, Kansas City guessed that Green Bay would try a running play. Surprise! Faking a "pitch" to running back Elijah Pitts, who pretended to carry the ball, drew many Chiefs defenders into the center of the action. Meanwhile, quarterback Bart Starr hooked up with Carroll Dale on a pass play topping 60 yards. Dale sprinted for a touchdown, only to see the score canceled because Green Bay was offside. Though Dale caught 438 passes from 1960–1973, including 52 touchdowns, he is perhaps best remembered for his part in this play that never was.

The Packers' Max McGee had a very good day in the January 1967 Super Bowl I. He caught two touchdown passes in the game, helping the Packers to a 35–10 win over the Kansas City Chiefs.

TAKE TO THE AIR

Starr recalled, "There was nothing I loved more than throwing long on third-and-short or fourth-and-short, when it was even more effective because of our conservative image." Usually, the Packers favored a run to gain only needed yardage, heading for a score in short bursts. "Play-action passing," the pass designed to look like a run, was one of their favorite methods for success. "Another reason we had success with long passes on short-yardage plays is that defenses knew that my passes were typically in the middle to short range," Starr said. "They thought I wasn't strong enough to throw it very deep."

Some teams will stick with success, if they see their quarterback has a favorite receiver, or if a running back stays unstoppable. But remember—the biggest surprises come when you're expecting something else. When football fans expect the unexpected, they will never be let down.

Today's quarterbacks aren't as fat as they look. Many wear padded rib protectors under jerseys. Some teams call them "flak jackets," a military term for bullet-proof vests.

7 STOP EVERYTHING

Mind, not just muscle, matters to today's pro football defenses. John Offerdahl was a Miami Dolphins linebacker from 1986 to 1993. In 89 games he recorded four interceptions and 9.5 quarterback sacks. (The half came when he and a teammate "shared" a sack.) Offerdahl explained today's defenses in the NFL: "Defensive plays are called through hand signals from the defensive coordinator," he said. "The defensive captain, usually the middle linebacker or safety, will translate the signal into a verbal command that is communicated in the huddle."

Out of the huddle, the defense takes their places on the line of scrimmage. But even before the ball is snapped, all 11 defenders can move, as long as they don't touch an offensive player across the line of scrimmage, the spot on the field where the ball has been put into play.

"Once [the defensive play is] called, the linebackers and safeties have the responsibility to alter the defense according to the offensive formation the opposing team comes to the line of scrimmage with," Offerdahl continued.

This gives the defense a slight advantage because, aside from receivers "in motion" running a short pattern behind the line of scrimmage, all other offensive players must not move until the ball is snapped. Moving gives the offense a "false start," with a penalty of playing the down over again, 5 yards back.

"Clear communication between the defensive backfield and line-backers becomes extremely important for good, sound defensive continuity," Offerdahl said.

PLAYING BY THE (PLAY)BOOK

Steve McMichael was a defensive lineman for three teams in 15 years, helping the Bears to a Super Bowl XX title. "I always considered myself a team player. I sacrificed a lot to go out there and do my job within the framework within the defenses that were called," he said. "I didn't go out there and try to freelance. I went out there and did the plays that came [down] to me. I think it's a big mistake when players go out there and run their own plays. When one player breaks down on defense, the whole unit goes to pot."

Linebacker Derrick Brooks of the Tampa Bay Buccaneers agreed, saying: "Statistics can be very misleading. My success was determined by what other players did around me to help me make plays."

Brooks continued, "When you line up, you block and you tackle. That is going to be the same whether you are playing little league, college, or professional. The fundamentals are just a thinking man's game. The higher you get, the more you have to think."

> **David "Deacon" Jones,** a star defensive end with the 1960s Los Angeles Rams, invented the term "sack" for tackling a quarterback before the ball was passed. Legend has it Jones told a reporter he'd like to tackle all QBs so hard that the team would need a sack to pick up the pieces.

IS BIGGER BETTER?

Brooks's coach, Tony Dungy, praised his player by saying, "Any defensive coach will take a smaller guy with speed, rather than a big guy who's slow." Brooks is "smaller," at 6 feet tall and 229 pounds. But Coach Dungy said, "He is smart. His greatest assets are his ability to learn something new and his quickness."

But what about size? Former Miami Dolphin Offerdahl, like most linebackers, faced some huge offensive linemen in his day. Surprisingly, he didn't believe that the biggest players are always the best at chasing quarterbacks. "A blitzing star [quarterback sack specialist] comes in all sizes, shapes, and speeds," Offerdahl said. "Equally as important as [physical] measurable skills is a knack for balance and leverage on an opposing offensive lineman. Hand strength and quickness [are] the pass rusher's most valuable weapon[s]."

Easier said than done? Offerdahl explained, "One who can successfully tap, swipe, or knock down the hands of an offensive lineman immediately negates the size and strength differential and now can expose the blocker's lack of speed as he pursues the quarterback."

> The 1970s became the decade of NFL team nicknames. The Minnesota Vikings defense was dubbed the "Purple People Eaters." The Pittsburgh Steelers defense was called the "Steel Curtain."

LITTLE BIG MAN

A star middle linebacker for Miami from 1969 to 1976 was Nick Buoniconti, a key to the Dolphins' unbeaten, Super Bowl-winning season in 1972. At 5 foot 11 and 220 pounds, Buoniconti was ignored by all 14 teams in the 1962 NFL draft due to concerns about his "small" size. He began his career with the Boston Patriots in the American Football League and displayed a work ethic that overshadowed his size. Even in practice, Buoniconti never hesitated. "Every play is like life and death," he told a reporter. "I can't think of anything except the play that is taking place at the moment."

Linebacker Derrick Brooks of the Tampa Bay Buccaneers in action against the San Francisco 49ers in a 1997 game. Brooks is known for his speed and agility.

One reason for that "life and death" feeling is that the pass rush has become the staple of current NFL defenses. As defensive coordinator of the Bears, Buddy Ryan reinvented the blitz. His "46" defense featured eight defenders bunched up front. The defense got its name because Chicago's free safety Doug Plank, wearing number 46, would move near the line's center, taking the middle linebacker's place on the field. In 1984 the team tallied a record 72 quarterback sacks. Chicago won Super Bowl XX, inspiring other clubs to create their own blitzing attacks.

SHARING THE GLORY

Linebacker Ted Hendricks, a 6-foot-7 defender nicknamed "The Mad Stork," explained the teamwork aspects of defense. "I don't care who you are or what you've done—in football, your success is a direct result of the personnel beside you. I had some great teammates and sometimes their job was to hold the guy up so I could make the play. You see some guys on TV now [tackle a] running back for a loss [of yardage] near the sideline, and instantly he holds his hands up like he's done something [great].

"The guy who knocked the pulling guard down to the ground so that the running back could be exposed is the one who should have his hands raised. It's a team game, and always will be."

The last, best hope of any defense is its backfield. Off the line of scrimmage, two cornerbacks (playing the corners past the line), a strong safety (who usually guards the offense's side where the tight end lines up), and a free safety (near the middle of the field, deepest among all defenders) guard against big plays. Deep-back players tail pass receivers on their routes and patterns. Pass coverage might be man-to-man (guarding specific receivers), zone (defending certain areas of the field, in case the play comes there), or double (more than one defender guarding a particularly tough receiver).

In Super Bowl VII, Miami kicker Garo Yepremian's field goal was blocked by 6-foot-5 Bill Brundige. Shocking some 90,000 fans, the

Part of a winning strategy may be the development of skill players, such as a player whose job it is to sack the quarterback. Broncos Neil Smith (right) has broken through the defense and has reached Packers quarterback Brett Favre before he can release the ball.

5-foot-8 Yepremian tried to pass the loose ball. Washington's 6-foot defensive end Mike Bass outreached, and outran, the kicker. Bass's 49-yard return dash gave the Redskins their only touchdown, even though the Dolphins won the championship, 14–7.

Whether facing the pass or a run, current defenses act first and react second. With speed and surprise, defenders hope to do more than limit an offensive play. The best defense will stop the play from ever happening.

Mental Games

The Denver Broncos were due in the tunnel soon—the tunnel to the field where 68,912 fans were waiting to watch Super Bowl XXXII on Sunday, January 25, 1998. The team had just a few minutes left in the locker room, minutes that coaches use to fire up teams by giving orders, instructions, and inspiring speeches.

Coach Shanahan led his players in the Lord's Prayer. Then he looked at their waiting faces. "Let's go out and show what kind of football team we have," he said. And that was all.

What kind of team did they have? The *Denver Post*, the Broncos' hometown newspaper, predicted that the team would lose the Super Bowl by a huge 31–17. Why not? Green Bay had won it all the previous year, and Denver hadn't even made it to the finals. Even this year, the Broncos hadn't won a title. They were at the Super Bowl as a "wild card."

Green Bay had more than a division trophy. They had quarterback Brett Favre, who had won his first-ever Super Bowl in 1997. Denver's John Elway had been in three Super Bowls when he was as young as Favre—and lost every one. Super Bowl XXXII might be the 37-year-old Elway's last chance for a championship ring, and everybody knew it.

Elway had the first 15 plays of his game plan memorized. Favre had his first 15, too. The preparation paid off for Green Bay. Commanding the first drive, Favre's game went exactly according to plan, right up to

The coin toss at the start of Super Bowl XXXII on January 25, 1998. In this clash of titans, John Elway and his Denver Broncos confronted Brett Favre and his Green Bay Packers.

the clean touchdown just four minutes into the game. Favre passed for 48 yards, telling Denver that Green Bay was relying on its quarterback's mighty arm.

Green Bay's defense took the field now. They looked like teachers on a playground, and the Broncos' offense were the kids. The four Packers up front weighed an average of 305 pounds each, the heaviest defensive line in the NFL. The Denver offensive linemen facing them were the league's lightest.

BRONCOS BUCK BACK

But Elway's game plan played out perfectly, too, including Denver's first touchdown. And Green Bay knew from running back Terrell Davis's thrilling 27-yard rush that the Broncos were going to rely on speed, especially Davis's. "They ran away from us," Packer cornerback Doug Evans told a reporter. If you saw 352-pound Packer Gilbert Brown coming at you, you would probably run away, too.

For the first time in Super Bowl history, each team scored a touchdown the first time they had the ball. Both teams had used their first drives to size up each other. Now the real battle could begin.

Favre launched Green Bay's next drive with a long, elegant pass. Denver was waiting for it: Tyrone Braxton intercepted, and the rush was on. The next play went to Davis for a 16-yard run. Just like before, another handoff to Davis pushed the Broncos closer to the goal line. Again to Davis—Green Bay was waiting for it. That's why Elway faked a handoff up the middle, kept the ball himself, and sprinted around the end of the line for Denver's second touchdown.

GROUND GAINER GOES

The second quarter swung Green Bay's way again. Terrell Davis left the game with a migraine headache. Elway threw more passes with Davis gone, and that meant his offensive line had to work harder to give him time to spot receivers. But even double-teaming didn't stop Green Bay's Gilbert Brown; two Broncos charging him barely slowed his steps. Denver only managed a field goal in the second quarter, but Green Bay defensive tackle Santana Dotson wasn't pleased with the way his team handled Denver's offense that day.

"We knew . . . how they were going to try to block us," he told *USA TODAY*, "and they did. They attacked us by cut-blocking us," blocking from an angle instead of straight on. "The main thing" that Dotson worried about "was their blocking technique and Terrell's ability to find the hole" in the Packers' formations.

Terrell Davis was back after halftime, his headache tamed. But the first thing he did was fumble. Good for Green Bay—a Packers field goal resulted, tying the game. But Denver undid the damage on the next possession. Elway shifted his passing game into high gear, throwing the Broncos close enough to taste a touchdown.

BRONCOS RUN WILD

Green Bay defensive coordinator Fritz Shurmur told the *Denver Post* that he had seen this tactic from other teams, where "their whole idea was to start with the passing game, and when you're forced to defend with more people out of the box than normally, then they'd pump the run at you."

Sure enough, Davis ran the ball 2 yards for his second touchdown, dragging Green Bay's number 55 with him.

Penalties and interceptions frustrated Green Bay more and more. "This is an offense built around Brett Favre," Denver defensive coordinator Greg Robinson said—and Denver did its best not to give Favre a chance at the ball. Late in the third quarter, it only took Favre 4 plays to pass for 57 yards and tie the game at 24 at the top of the fourth quarter.

ONE LAST SCORE?

As the clock ticked down, both teams struggled. Denver lined up in the "slot" formation, running to the side that looked the least protected. That gave fleet-footed Davis a chance to do what he did best: find the holes and run right through them. Green Bay's defense was getting tired because Denver was controlling the ball. Denver even found a way to block big Gilbert Brown—in the double team, one Bronco went high, the other went low, and Brown didn't go anywhere.

With barely a minute and a half left in the game, Denver was at the 1-yard line with a first down. Desperate, Green Bay chose a bizarre strategy: "Our defense let those guys score right there at the end so we could have some time," Favre told *USA TODAY*.

"It was the only sensible thing to do," safety LeRoy Butler agreed. Spending too much time trying to stop a Denver score would run the clock down, leaving Green Bay no time to score again.

PACKING IT IN

Now the score was Denver 31, Green Bay 24, with 1:48 left. The Broncos knew that if anyone could turn around a situation like this, it was Packers quarterback Favre. They defended tightly against Favre's passes until, on Green Bay's fourth down, Denver's John Mobley knocked down Favre's last attempt, from the 31-yard line with 28 seconds left. Time had run out for the Packers. Denver was the new Super Bowl champion.

"We were just trying to make a play at the end of a game," Favre tried to explain later. "If the play works, then it's a great call. If it

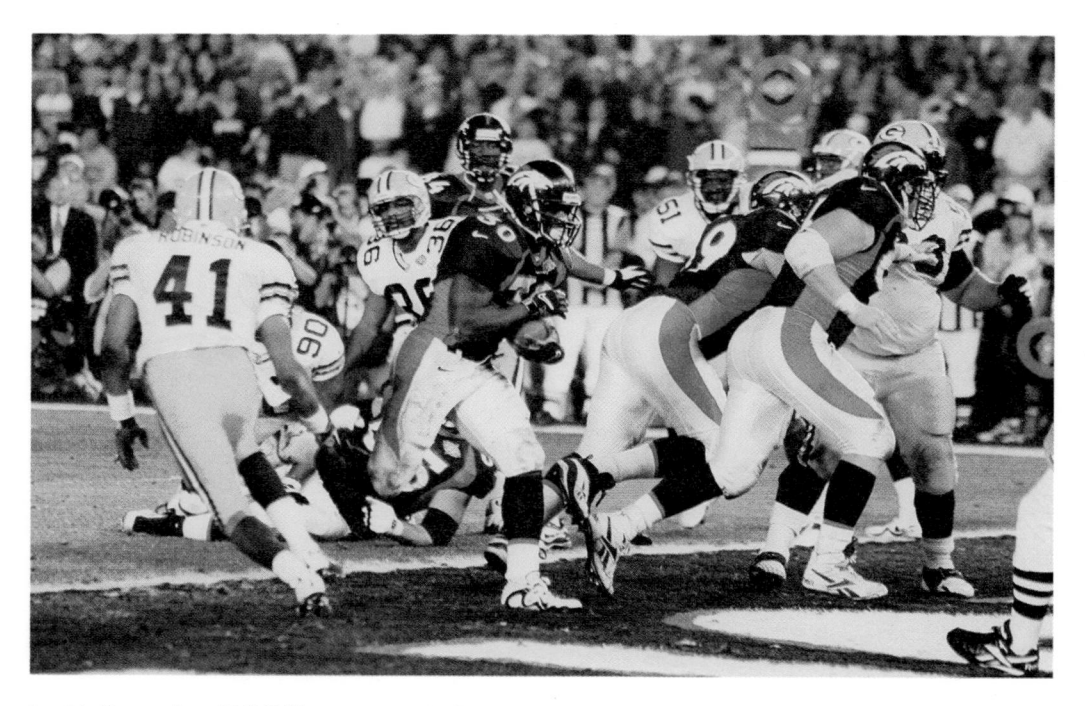

In this Super Bowl XXXII game action, Broncos running back Terrell Davis charges through a gap in the Packers defense to score the winning touchdown late in the fourth quarter. Davis was named the game MVP.

doesn't, then we should have called something else. We called what we thought was our best stuff, and we did not take advantage of it."

Strategy means taking chances, trying what you think is best and executing it the best you can. But there's a part of strategy that cannot be planned.

John Elway, who'd won more games than any other quarterback in history but lost three Super Bowls, said, "No matter what you do, if you've never won a Super Bowl, that's what's mentioned first."

Sometimes, all that strategy boils down to is who wants the win most. That can't be planned.

Or can it?

The culmination of a successful game plan—the Broncos hold up the Vince Lombardi trophy they won in Super Bowl XXXII.

THE BRONCOS' WINNING ATTITUDE

For the two weeks before the game, Denver players had followed Coach Shanahan's instructions: They didn't brag, they didn't compare teams, they even told the press how much they respected Green Bay.

Bronco Bill Romanowski told NBC, "We knew we were the better team. But we sucked up to (Green Bay) for two weeks. I was so sick of telling them how good they were, I wanted to puke. But we did it."

Announcer Joe Gibbs, who had coached the Washington Redskins to three Super Bowls, called the Broncos' pregame tactic "one of the keys of the game."

Denver's Gary Zimmerman said, "When you hear that for two weeks, it kind of builds a fire under you. We had to sit quiet and bite our tongues, and that was a hard thing to do. It's been brewing in our stomachs every night, and deep in our hearts we knew we could do it. We were just waiting till Sunday to prove it."

That, Gibbs said, was the game plan.

> The top ticket for the first Super Bowl cost $12. Although 61,946 attended, some reporters were disappointed. The game was held in the Los Angeles Coliseum, which could have held 90,000 fans.

GLOSSARY

audible a change of play by a quarterback at the line of scrimmage, telling his offense to cancel the original play and use a different one. This happens when the defense has left a good opening, or when the defense seems too well prepared for the upcoming offense. To keep the defense from figuring out the audible signal, the quarterback sometimes calls fake, or dummy, audibles.

blitz a defensive tactic in which one or more linebackers or backs rush at the quarterback. It could result in a sack or a bad pass.

block to stop an opponent by getting in the way. Grabbing (see **holding**) or blocking from behind (see **clipping**) is illegal.

clipping an illegal block whereby a player hits an opponent in the back.

combination coverage use of man-to-man defense on one side of the field and zone defense on the other. (See **man-to-man** and **zone**.)

conversion an attempt by the team that just scored a touchdown to add one point by place-kicking the ball between the goalposts, or two points by running or passing the ball from the two-yard line into the end zone in one play. (See **extra point**.)

cornerback a defensive position. Cornerbacks try to keep receivers from catching the ball, and tackle ball carriers who get past the linebackers.

defense a team of players who try to keep the offensive team from scoring.

defensive back a back who plays behind the defensive line and linebackers and is responsible for stopping pass completions. (See **secondary, cornerback,** and **safety**.)

defensive line the first row of defensive players on the line of scrimmage, usually tackles and ends. Their job is to stop the run and the quarterback.

down a play. The team with the ball gets four downs to move the ball 10 yards. If 10 yards are gained in less than four plays, the count of four starts again.

end zone the 10 yards from the goal line to the goal post, which is the end of the playing field. The two end zones are not included in the 100 yards of the regular field.

extra point a point that may be earned by the team that just scored a touchdown, by hiking the ball from the two-yard line and place-kicking it through the goal posts. (See **conversion**.)

field goal a place-kick, worth three points.

first down the first of four downs that may be used to gain 10 yards. If the required yardage is not reached on the first down, the team is allowed three additional downs.

flea-flicker in early football games, this play was a pass reception, followed by the receiver lateraling the ball to a nearby teammate. Now the play has many variations, all behind the line of scrimmage. One common flea-flicker is a handoff to a running back, who laterals back to the quarterback for a surprise pass.

fumble loss of control of the ball. Either team may grab the free ball and try to advance it toward a score.

goal line a white line at each end of the 100-yard field. Points are scored by advancing the ball over the other team's goal line.

handoff a play in which the running back is handed the ball by the quarterback.

holding blocking by grabbing illegally.

huddle a gathering of players on the same team to plan what to do for the next play.

incomplete pass a pass that is not caught by anyone on offense or defense.

inside toward the center of the playing field.

interception the catch of a pass by a member of the defensive team.

kickoff a placekick to the other team that begins each half of a game, and follows any scoring.

linebackers the second line of defensive players. They back the defensive line.

line of scrimmage   the place on a field where a play begins. Offensive players line up facing the goal they are driving toward. Defensive players face the offense. The line of scrimmage can be anywhere on the field except the end zones.

man-to-man   a defensive alignment whereby a player is assigned one offensive player to cover. The defensive player will follow his man anywhere. (See also **zone** and **combination**).

offense   players on the team with possession of the ball, trying to score.

offensive line   the first offensive players at the line of scrimmage, usually a center, two guards, and two tackles. Their job is to protect the quarterback and block for running backs.

outside   toward the sidelines of the playing field.

passing game   a strategy that relies on throwing the ball.

penalty   a loss of yardage or a down for doing something illegal.

placekick   a kick of a ball held by another player or placed in a special holder called a tee; the kicker runs up and kicks the ball. (See **extra point, field goal,** and **kickoff.**)

pocket   an area of the backfield guarded by the offensive line to protect the quarterback against charging defensive players.

practice squad   players who practice with teammates but don't play during actual games.

punt   kicking the ball without a tee. The kicker drops the ball himself and kicks it before it touches the ground.

quarterback   the offensive player who starts almost every play by receiving the ball from the center. The quarterback relays the coach's assigned play in the huddle. At the line of scrimmage, the quarterback reads the two teams' positions, then starts the play by either calling the assignment or an audible. After receiving the ball, the quarterback either runs with it, hands it off, or passes it to a teammate. (See **read, audible.**)

read   to look at where opposing players are and use that information to guess what they are about to do.

reception   the catch of a pass from a teammate, usually the quarterback.

red zone   the 20 yards of the field before the end zone. The red zone is not marked off. Whenever a team is within 20 yards of scoring a touchdown, they are said to be in the red zone.

return   to run with a ball that has been kicked, punted, fumbled, or intercepted.

running back   an offensive back who carries the ball.

running game   a strategy that relies on running with the ball.

rush   to run with the ball on offense, or to pressure the quarterback on defense.

sack   to tackle the quarterback behind the line of scrimmage.

safety   1. the defensive player farthest behind the line of scrimmage. The safety is responsible for stopping any offensive play that has gotten past the rest of his team. 2. Two points gained by the defensive team for tackling an offensive player or causing the offense to commit a penalty in the offensive end zone.

scramble   to run with the ball, as a quarterback, to evade onrushing defensive players.

scrimmage   1. a meeting or encounter. (See **line of scrimmage**.) 2. a practice game, sometimes among teammates.

secondary   see **defensive back**.

slot formation   an offensive formation with a receiver positioned in a "slot" in the backfield behind the main offensive line, between the tackle and end.

snap   the beginning of each play, where the center passes the ball under his body and between his legs to another player, usually the quarterback.

special teams   players involved primarily in kicking plays, such as kickoffs, punts, or field goals. Some of them also play in other play situations.

tight end   the offensive player who alternately blocks for the quarterback or running back and receives passes, staying close to the offensive line.

touchdown   the act of scoring by running or throwing the ball safely into the end zone; it is worth six points, the most that can be earned at once.

wide receiver   an offensive player who takes a position away from the offensive line to catch passes.

wild card   a team that still makes the playoffs, even without winning the division. Each year, three teams from each conference get "wild card" spots in the playoffs.

yard line   any line that crosses the field from sideline to sideline. Actual yard lines are marked every five yards; plays that stop in between are measured off during the game.

zone   an area of the field assigned to a defender to protect against advances by offensive players there.

FOR MORE INFORMATION

Books

Converse staff. *Converse 3 All-Star Football: How to Play Like a Pro.* New York: Wiley, 1996.

Gutman, Bill. *The Kids' World Almanac of Football.* Mahwah, NJ: World Almanac Books, 1994.

Poling, Jerry. *Untold Stories of the Green Bay Packers.* Madison, WI: Prairie Oak Press, 1996.

Riggins, John and Jack Winter. *Gameplan: The Language & Strategy of Pro Football.* Santa Barbara: Santa Barbara Press, 1984

Books for Older Readers

Didinger, Ray, ed. *Game Plans for Success: Winning Strategies for Business and Life from 10 Top NFL Head Coaches.* Chicago: Contemporary Books, 1995.

Gibbs, Joe, with Jerry Jenkins. *Fourth and One.* Nashville: Thomas Nelson Publishers, 1991.

Green, Tim. *The Dark Side of the Game: My Life in the NFL.* New York: Warner Books, 1996.

Montana, Joe with Richard Weiner. *Joe Montana's Art and Magic of Quarterbacking.* New York: Henry Holt, 1997.

Peary, Danny. *Super Bowl: The Game of Their Lives.* New York: Macmillan, 1997.

Theismann, Joe with Brian Tarcy. *The Complete Idiot's Guide to Understanding Football Like a Pro.* New York: Alpha Books/Macmillan, 1997.

Total Football. Edited by Bob Carroll, Michael Gershman, David Neft, John Thorn. New York: HarperCollins, 1997.

Internet Resources

www.nfl.com
This is the official National Football League Web site.

www.canton-ohio.com/hof/
Want to visit the Football Hall of Fame from your computer?

www.usatoday.com/sports/nfl.htm
Many media Web sites offer updated daily news on the NFL. This newspaper is an all-star at offering the most football news the fastest.

INDEX